It's all Bull honky: We must question everything!

Bobby Simonds

ISBN: 9798638534783

ISBN 13: XXXXX

Library of Congress Control Number: XXXXX

LCCN Imprint Name: Independently published

https://www.amazon.com/bobbysimonds

Front Cover & Editing by author.

Contacts & Hashtags:

bobby.simonds@gmail.com

www.facebook.com/bobbyraysimonds

www.facebook.com/bobbyrsimonds

www.instagram.com/@bobbysimonds

#bobbyraysimonds

#bobbysimonds

#BOBBYRAYSIMONDS

#ATWISTINTRAVEL

#risenfromtheashes

#toxicamerica

#Challenge-thyself

#avoidinghavoc

#bobbyscreativephotographyseries

#QUESTIONINGREALITY

#thedoctorscall

#evilmatters

#pandorasbox

#everythingchangeswithbrainsurgery

#UnfoldingMisery

#therealjerrylewis

#itsallbullhonky

#questioneverything

As a self-taught author, I spend much time researching many various topics. This could very well include current events, current conspiracies, and current conspiracy gossip (which I put a spin on that name).

Between using Google & Youtube; one could easily lose themselves in this long, and eventful lavish web.

I have created/published many books; which with my nonfiction, I have more than enough proof, which I can not only keep up with current events, but years later, my books seem to stay up-to-date.

Like many authors before me, I too, am exceptionally observant. I am also intrigued with the successful, mindset of being an international author, and as I continue to write, my books become more successful because of people like you, who took a chance on something new, and original to read!

I was born with Mild Cerebral Palsy, and have had brain surgery. Which, I do not allow either to slow me down, and/or get in my way. I do not compare myself to other authors, however, I do believe I have what it takes.

Booklovers connect with me from my own personal biography. Connecting with readers on more of an emotional level; I decided to include topics such as: inner healing, conspiracy, grievance, political, suicide, & finishing up with positive outcomes.

On a side note, I have assisted others to glorify their dream, by directing them with the essentials for writing, and the publishing tools, that they would need, of course.

I've soared over topics such as, social media, "fake news," UFOs, the Alien Conspiracy, "mythical" creatures, religion, politics, cloning, life-sucking tablets. Furthermore, in one book, I even predicted Donald Trumps' win, before he was even close to upsetting Hilary Clinton's supporters.

As far as my fiction books go, I must say that I am still in the process of enjoying a world to create for my readers to escape their normal bubble, to enjoy somebody else's insanity. I currently only have one true novel, and the rest being, labeled as 'novella's' or short stories. Majority of my books, both fiction & nonfiction, generally are series. Obviously, I wrote a few individuals, but I prefer the other choice.

I hope that you are brave enough to leave your review of what you had thought of with this book, and others. Whether you are a previous supporter of mine, or a new one, be respectful and leave a review where you had purchased this book. Thanks for your participation, and I look forward to reading your review, or messages to me.
In addition, I hope you (the reader) check back on Amazon.com (or whatever link you purchased my titles), monthly, because I tend to publish a minimum of 5 books per year. Majority of the time, it's more realistically 10 books per year.

Dedication

I dedicate this book to all of you, whom are conspiracy theorists. To believe in something so strongly, by not letting anyone talk you out of something, is a true belief. And, it takes brass nuts, to stay strong, when there are so many that don't understand what's truly in their reality.

[14]

<u>**What is the definition of bull honky?**</u>

*Noun – Uncountable. Nonsense. Lies.
Literally, bull feces.*

*A word used by gangbangers (yeah, okay).
It can be describe someone, and it is used
instead of "bullshit."*

*Sad to say, it's also a company that makes
winter hoodies – Bullhonky Deluxe…!*

Chapter 1

The world has changed, drastically. There isn't anything we could do about our current circumstances, except for staying indoors, as much as possible – so it seems.

With the roads clearing from traffic, from nearly everyone out of work; I wonder if it will be like the old days? Back when Columbus first encounter *America – first known as, the New World.*

It is said by Indians (old & new generations), that there were creatures of "unknown" origins, that roamed cautiously

before the British had "re-discovered" America.

Henry Hudson (who named the Hudson

River) was said to encounter fairies. He didn't

recall how he entered the 'fairy world,' but

what seemed like only a few hours, were in

fact, a few weeks.

Both Henry Hudson & Christopher

Columbus were among the first to record seeing

Mermaids, during their travels from England to

America, too. Shakespeare was another.

The following (short) list, is said to be

reported by many, who first came to settle in

America. These are also, still being witnessed today.

1) Giants

2) Trolls

3) Satyrs

4) Faeries (fairies)

5) Mermaids/mermen

6) Elves

7) Centaurs

8) Ghosts

9) Bigfoot (of course)

10) Aliens

11) Werewolves

12) Pukwudgie (found mainly in

Delaware)

13) St. Augustine Monster (first

discovered in 1896, in Florida. Looks

like an octopus)

14) Piasa (found along the Mississippi

River, by Native Americans)

15) Pope Lick Monster (basically a

goat/sheep/man, found in Kentucky)

16) Dewayyo (found in Maryland, said

to be a flying blood sucker, like a

wolf or coyote body, with wings)

17) Red Dwarf (found in Michigan,

basically an evil Leprechaun)

18) Wendigo (found in Great Lakes
Regions)

19) Jersey Devil (flying, hoofed
creature that prey's on stranded
humans in New Jersey)

20) Reptilians (found in both nature
and desert regions around the globe;
it's said that they live in tunnels under
our world)

Obviously, my personal top 20-list,
carries a ton of conspiracy, by many. Me,
personally, I find the said list to be quite
accurate, with being witnessed in America.

[21]

There have been hundreds, and even thousands

of reports with this list; and it seems there are

much more, of course. However, we would

have had more reports, if we didn't have so

many distractions from even spotting these

various creatures.

Before the Corona-virus pandemic, we

had many motorists on the road, which, when

you figure majority of the time, we're drinking

our beverages, eating food, talking on the

phone, and even listening to music – all while

we drive, or ride in the vehicle. We're not

concentrating what's that 'shadow' in the

bushes. Except, perhaps, while it's pitch-black

outside, and our awareness is heightened.

[23]

Chapter 2

In April of 2020 – Utica, New York,
there has been more Orange, Orb sightings.
Obviously, once it becomes a public post, you
will see the first few comments being "weather
balloons" mentioned. It's a given these days.
Nonetheless, I have seen them in the past, with
my own eyes, and hundreds of witnesses. I've
written about these experiences & observations
in past books, even. However, it seems that
they are becoming more frequent since
everyone was highly recommended to "self-
quarantine."

Last night (April 13,2020), I was outside

smoking, everything was dead silent. I didn't

even hear the geese in the nearby swamp

making their nightly noises – to keep predators

away. I found it odd, since there hasn't been a

night that goes by, without hearing them since

the middle of March.

I shrugged it off, assuming that it was my

mind playing tricks on me, since I was tired,

and it was approaching midnight.

Suddenly, I instantly got goosebumps in

the back of my neck, and my arms, too. Then, I

heard it, a noise I haven't heard since I lived in

California. The sounds of a Reptilian. I didn't

see it, but I did pinpoint the location; just

behind a tree, not 100 feet, from me. I knew

that it knew, I heard it. It didn't murmur the

noise.

I cautiously finished my cigarette, and

slowly entered my home. The chills racing up

and down my body like a racetrack, put me on

edge.

I returned swiftly to my office. I

researched titles for my next book (this one), on

Amazon, and didn't find anything that matches.

I was astounded, and excited, simultaneously. I

went back onto my game, and attempted to

occupy my mind, but it didn't work. I

continuously had flashes of what the creature would look like. I couldn't focus on the body, per say. However, I had a clear image of it's head, and its hands, wrapping it's fingers and claws around the tree bark; watching me; observing me… It was creepy. That is one species you don't want to encounter. They are predators. However, even though that it scared the wits out of me, I strongly believe it meant me no harm. Only, it was specifically there, perhaps, passing thru, and it saw me, along its journey. Instead of instigating terror, it was merely an observation. I know for certain that it was, alone.

This scenario, is exactly what I am referring to, with the majority being at home, quietly. Extraterrestrial beings, and dimensional beings are roaming our world, more freely, so it seems.

Between the sky and the land, you'll never truly know what to expect that goes,

bump in the night.

Chapter 3

In my last two books, I had serious issues with Amazon publishing them. A 2-part series (so far), sold over 100 copies in the first week of publication. Amazon won't allow me to publish volume 2 of "Invisible War", because it 'insinuates' a non-scientific look at the virus. Further, I believe that their algorithm has been upgraded just before business closures, to keep people from telling the truth. God forbid, we speak the truth as writers!

In *Invisible War: The Coronavirus Reality,* I wrote quickly about the business closures, and the possibility of seeing Marshall Law. I never once said that it would happen, only that it could. In the sequel, *Invisible War: Failure to Win*, I wrote about the stupidity with people not taking precautions seriously, nor the proper procedures with both wearing masks, gloves, and even social distancing (staying six feet away from another human).

Explain how this is a reason to ban both books? It literally took me 4 times to publish the first, and I was able to publish both e-book & paperback. The second, they refuse to publish a paperback, even though they allowed the e-book to become published (after 5 times).

Their excuse? The felt that I was misleading

readers that I was a medical expert, and refuse

to allow a paperback to be published. When I

inquired why they would allow the e-book thru,

and not the paperback, their only response was,

"we stick by our original decision with not

allowing the paperback to be published." What

sorta *bull honky* is that?

In order, to make it as an author –

especially, when creating nonfiction – you must

always speak the <u>truth</u> to the best of your

ability. You <u>must</u> always ensure to your

readers that you are looking out for <u>their best</u>

<u>interests</u>, not the publishers, or third parties –

that may publish you, with using algorithms,' not actual human, eyes!

Speaking of truth, I have been paying attention to the latest conspiracy theories with our current pandemic crisis. *Long time author & researcher, David Icke (of England)*, had been discussing both the *5G conspiracy*, along with *frequencies*. He has a very fascinating mind, as many would agree. In his latest post, he discusses the *Perception Frequencies*. What he means by that, is that our perception is being altered by everything we do. Everything we see, we use, Virtual Reality, Smartphones, Social Media, commercials, and much more. I totally agree with this, because I've written similar theories – I didn't say/claim, frequencies, but my intentions with writing about VR and smartphones, commercial ads, and much more, all had to do with this. Apparently, I was on to something!

Anyhow, with David's theory, he mentions with everyone's perception being altered, we aren't seeing our own reality. Which, brings me to my theory. My theory is this, if our perceptions are being altered daily, and our education is being obscured by real education, then this would explain why there are so many skeptics. Further, if you can't contemplate a flying, orange orb, then how can

you contemplate seeing an alien-entity, right

smack, in front of your eyes?

[37]

Chapter 4

There are many conspiracy theories surrounding 5G. One of the most recent, is part of the cause of our current pandemic. They claim that there are two sources for the extreme breaching of the virus. One being administered directly with humans, and the other thru the 5G towers, around the globe.

If you were to consider how outlandish this sounds, it's not all that extreme. A virus can spread very quickly, if it's swept under the carpet, like it was in China, back in December of 2019. Nonetheless, the outward spread in just a couple of months is more than insanity.

Sure, the virus can jump from country to country, from international flights, as it was suggested. However, they claimed that in the beginning, it wasn't at all airborne. It was initially spread by surfaces, and even shoes. But, what if the 5G towers were activated during the beginning phase of the spread?

It is said that the 5G towers spread frequencies, which, can initiate the immunity within a persons body, which would welcome the virus. The bigger the city, more the towers.

There are ton in the country, too, but not nearly as widespread as in the city.

When the towers were first being rushed into being built, the workers became ill from the amount of radiation that came off the towers.

If humans are all on the same frequency, and the towers were able to tap into our human frequencies, then it would become a fact that these towers could weaken the immune system. Each person has a different result, as far as recovery or death.

Scientists have all concluded that the human soul is connected thru frequencies. This isn't new. However, governments across the globe have discovered that dispersing large crowds can be done by using certain radio frequencies. The internet, traffic signals, radio channels, satellites, cable television, and so much more, are all done by a specific frequency. They fill a space, and then by the push of a button, they are sent to us. We pay for these frequencies with services, like the internet and cable television (and satellites, too).

We may have never anticipated that these services would be used against us, only for entertainment and pleasure. It's no different than assuming our elect-governments would

intend to deceive the public, because we "didn't

sign-up" for it. But it occurs all the time. Sure,

the illusion with a democracy is best, because

without the democracy, humanity would surely

fail. That's no surprise, since it's always been

clear we need a 'leader' to ensure our survival,

as individuals, and as a race.

[43]

Chapter 5

I often wonder why people tell their children to stop using their "imaginations?" What if our so-called *imaginations* are something, everyone else isn't seeing, within their own reality?

Because, when they tell you to stop talking to your *imaginary friend*, there's generally something more to it, than imaginary. Many psychic's believe that these children who experience having an *imaginary friend* are in fact, communicating with a spirit. However, what if it is more than that? I know when I was

[44]

a child, my imaginary friend wasn't a spirit,

moreover, it was my alien friend. Other times,

it was a spirit guide, or what is now referred to

as, a mythical creature. Therefore, why are we

told that we're nuts that children are

experiencing having an imaginary friend,

exactly? Just because you don't see it for

yourself, doesn't mean there isn't there, with

your child!

The definition of *imagination* is as

follows: ***1) the faculty or action of forming***

new ideas, images or concepts of external

objects not present to the <u>senses</u>. 2) the ability

of the mind to be creative or resourceful.

That said, wouldn't the true meaning be something like, *seeing what others cannot, is believing?*

It makes perfect sense to me, but who am I to expect you to understand, fully?!

Many of us share a commonality. This being, we see shapes in clouds, trees, plants, bushes, snow banks, and many other things – even in the flooring of our homes.

What if these shapes, that many of us see as creatures, such as, horses, dragons, dogs, cats, passed loved ones, etc., are there? What if, they are reality, and our minds – being shaped as they were, from being raised in the

[46]

wrong schooling, and other forms of knowledge

- that we're fed much deception from the ages

of 4 and up… Can these images merely be our

minds deceiving **us**? While others are literally

claiming imagination? Perhaps, the simplistic

answer, must be: **YES**.

Chapter 6

Have you ever gained a strange glance at any given tree, sitting all by its lonesome? Only a questioning mind gives such a tree a second thought. Such questions could be expected, like, *damn, that tree really does look like a prop. Why is that tree all by itself? And, why isn't that tree with the forest, just sitting only a few hundred feet away?*

I have asked those very same questions, myself. Living outside the city, I am surrounded by nature, at any given time. And like the said questions above, there are many trees like that example (of said questions), that very much, look like props from a theatre setting – and even a movie.

Other things that may stand out to question your reality, too, would be random bushes, the utter, freakiness of silence – that literally, and randomly occurs in [or nearby] forests. The 'unexplained' occurs more frequently in nature, rather than, in the city regions. Small towns look like props from a bomb-test site, and the people are extremely different from big city folk.

The skies are more desolate, because you're not next to an international airport, or have police helicopters flying over with the

spotlight looking down on unsuspected citizens.

Traffic is usually dumb people, keeping the

same distance as the car next to them, and

breaking every chance they get. The attitude of

with work is a much slower paced, whether it's

busy, or not. Lastly, there are less camera's on

the street, from an obvious standpoint.

With all that said, this is country living.

And it feels as though, that the FLAT EARTH

THEORY, seems more real, every day.

Furthermore, attached with the FLAT EARTH

THEORY, is living in a movie set, nearly

identical to the movie, *The Truman Show – Jim Carrey.*

There are many people that still believe the scientific community, that the earth is round, we *did* land on the moon [and other planets, such as Mars]. Nevertheless, if you live in a small town, it is easy to consider the possibility. Especially, when looking at things thru a visionary microscope. Meaning, your own set of eyes.

There are many people with an OCD syndrome, and I have it when it comes to looking at the 'reality' I live in. I've mentioned many times to my wife, *that tree looks just like a prop.* Then you touch it, and move the branches, and the brain from within, explains to you that it is real – because that is, after all, what school has brainwashed us.

We don't know that NASA has landed on the moon, put satellites in the sky, or even left the Earth's atmosphere. We only believe what they tell us, because they tell lies so damn well! Our tax money at waste, is brainwashing us away. There are just as many debunkers in the population, as conspiracy theories, and it's quite difficult (if you don't know how to trust your own intuition, and 'gut') to believe lies coming from the scientific community. Quite frankly, we hope that we aren't trapped in a Reality-like, movie studio.

Where do we learn history from? The internet, and school. And who teaches these so-called facts, of human history? Teachers, professors, which are taught from schools. Schools, which are assigned what to elaborate on subjects from the ones who rule our 'world.' It's all about order, and brainwashing.

In recent decades, there have been more and more people 'waking-up' to learn, and believe that the *Flat Earth Theory* isn't so much as a theory. There are hidden proofs, which, in various circles, reveal facts – not theories – just like the symbolism left behind from the

Freemasons (a.k.a., The Illuminati, & Skull &

Bones Secret Societies).

It doesn't really matter if you are a die-

hard skeptic, or an open-minded believer. It's

all about what you learn, and fighting what

your brain is conforming your mind to know,

because it was previously brainwashed into

'knowing' the earth is round, the sun is a ball of

fire, and the moon landing occurred before the

Russians, and the footage was viewed by

millions on a day in the 1960s!

I suppose it would be like seeing an alien

for the first time, or a flying saucer (a.k.a.,

UFO). Nonetheless, these things are real, and millions are coming forward with new evidence daily.

Furthermore, any government will express to their civilians that there is a space program, and they know how to manipulate the weather. They'll lie thru their teeth at first, but eventually they slip 'off-the-record,' which is then released on the internet.

We've never left 'earth' and we never will. Wars are created as a diversion for people to move on, to kill a flock of people, to keep the population down.

I've heard many stories of soldiers killing unarmed people, in villages – because their orders were claiming that they had 'arms-of-destruction' nearby, or inside the perimeter. Then, after they've killed unarmed civilians, they've found nothing threating. This isn't something new, it's been occurring since after, WWII.

To be honest, Hitler was most likely instructed by a secret society, to annihilate a race, to keep the population down. And, since the Jews were flagged, and White Supremacy was at the height of the war, it wouldn't surprise me any, if the orders were coming

from an alien, white race.

There are many circumstances with the

conspiracy of why Hitler did what he did, let

alone, survive at the end of the war in

Argentina. But that isn't what's in our schools

history books!

If we believed everything we were taught

in school, there would be more people believing

that dinosaurs roamed 'the earth,' the moon

landing occurred (oh, wait, they do believe

those two!). What people question, is Darwin's

Theory. Theories are merely speculation, not

fact. At least people got that one! Show me

[58]

one ape in the past century that transformed

into a human, just one!

Chapter 7

The healthcare isn't what it was when our grandparent's, or their grandparent's had sought medical attention. Shit, back then, doctors were known to make house calls!

The hospitals, clinics, and doctor's offices are all run as a cold business. You used to be able to take in a sheet of paper, with a list, now you are only allowed up to 5 things, and some, only 3.

Many American's want free healthcare. I say, the only way it should be free, is if NASA, NSA, HOMELAND SECURITY, FBI, CIA, many other various agencies are disbanded, closed, and free up the money, so health care would truly be free – along with living a TAX-FREE-LIFE!

However, these things won't occur. There's always a cost. Like Canada, for example. They have 'free' healthcare. But at what cost to them? Sixty percent of their checks go to the healthcare – that's not free!

In the city, there are hundreds, to thousands of cameras watching everything you do. Why? I once believed what the conspiracy theorists claimed – to watch every move you do; because *Big Brother* is watching. That's partly true, but I strongly believe it's to add to

the movie set.

Chapter 8

Living in a real motion picture is, well, strange. People would laugh at this notion. But seriously, you must consider it.

Every person has had this happen more than once in their life:

We've had times where we don't feel as though we are acting ourselves; it feels as though, we've lost complete control of our actions, watching from a distance, and something – or someone – has done something, or said something to another human. The after effect is strange. We either want to take back what was said, or the action that was done – because in

our reality, we wouldn't do or say those things;

even from anger.

    Now, with the notion & concept, which I sat in front of you, are you considering all the possibilities? With the upper hands controlling weather, relaying lies, upon lies, with leaving earth, and brainwashing people that it's factual evidence? Such as, a picture of earth, or satellites in the 'space,' just outside of earth's atmosphere? What about all the computer-generated images of other planets, or even stars? Have you ever noticed that the Sun, isn't what it seems, as far as, what we've been led to believe…You know, a burning fire of light? A.k.a., a star? Or, what about the moon? Both photography and videos from the past to the present, prove to everyone that it was all a hoax – made in some studio, presented to the world from none other than, Hollywood itself.

Yet, more than half of the world's population believes we've been to space, Mars, the Moon, and to the end of our universe, all because of *The Great Deception* put forth, to lead humans astray. People are obviously believing such foolish garbage. Perhaps, it is because they want to believe, that we're not stuck in a dome, floating somewhere in the

universe, in a spaceship?

Chapter 9

The picture I used for the cover, got me really thinking of the larger scheme of the world that we were once, all taught. *The earth is round; we're surrounded by desolate planets, that once sustained life. We went to the moon, but haven't been back since. The world is run by a select-elite, secret society, that only they, know the truth & reality of which we were all born into.*

But if this were all truths, hidden behind the microscope of life, then why have there been so many theories, given by authors, professors, and even scientists throughout

history, based on the concept of both a false-

reality, and that the Earth is either a dome, or a

spaceship?

The concepts are more hints to learn the

false-reality, that we were led to believe that we

have been here since the extinction of

dinosaurs. But what if the dinosaurs never

became extinct, but moved into another

dimension, only a few shareholders have been

able to visit (and/or, determine)?

With the way the winter storms have

been for the past twenty, or even thirty years, it

makes perfect sense to me, that we not only live

in a simulated-reality, but the possibility of a dome-earth (flat earth/dome concept), inside of a spaceship, is becoming quite apparent to me. Not from listening, or even reading others before me, who have thought of these theories. But that it would make perfect sense. Mainly, if you look at the larger picture of things. Such being, our history with humanity.

People are so focused on the little things, that grew into larger things from historical drawings from caves, or books even. Nonetheless, this is only what we're told about our past. Many depictions in Egypt have proven that 'man' had prior knowledge with space suits.

The scientific/archeology communities all claim that these depictions with entities wearing space suits were known as *Gods* from *space*. But what if, they wore them in our own 'planet' because the air may have been toxic to them? They may have technological advances that 'humans' never had during those times, and these beings simply came from either another dimension on "Earth," or a secret land that is on Earth, that normal humans aren't allowed the sacred knowledge?

I was watching a Youtube video the other day, which had to do with "Earth is a Spaceship." And, no, it was Disney's white-looking Golf ball, which they called, *Spaceship Earth*. No, this was a serious theory, not just about flat earth, but the person behind the video came up with a great theory. This theory showed his concept that Earth has a cutoff point in Antarctica, and just on the other side, a whole new 'world' with vast lands/continents, just like our 'world.' Then, the illustration used, also revealed that 'Earth' lay on a type of asteroid, floating thru Space; which also, had an invisible-like dome over our 'planet.' It was fascinating. Furthermore, I viewed this video after I began writing my own theories based on the topic, without even knowing that there were others before me, considering this huge possibility.

I find it to be ironic, that every time a virtuous concept/theory comes into play, it is covered-up with creating a fictional solution. Such as movies, rides to a theme park, or something else that leads you in a different direction, when doing an online search. They clearly don't want you to pay attention to these theories, because they are too close to the truth.

They want you to follow their deceptions, no matter the cost. But, to be honest with you, it changes nothing. Even if you were to believe, it's just simply for knowledge, because nothing will be changed, to keep the crew in order.

If you were to consider a crew on a spaceship, or a regular ship, everyone has a job to do – even if you are a passenger. The passenger's job duties are to include entertainment and relaxation. The crew members is to keep order, food, beverages, cleaning of every kind, entertainment, and pretty much everything we do already.

[77]

Chapter 10

I have a pretty strong theory, with why,

we have always been deceived. My theory is

like when the doors get locked from the

outside, and the masses are trapped inside of a

building. What occurs to these people?

PANIC. Panic takes over, and people get hurt,

and people could also die.

My theory, is most likely fact.

Nonetheless, it is what it is. Things occur over

time, and lies build, and the truth cannot be

told, because then, they'd have to explain every

lie, ever told to the masses. And this isn't

something that just began, it's from the

beginning of humanity, until present day. Just

like the *Alien Cover-ups, Area 51, 9/11, JFK*

assignation, and even The Roswell Incident.

What seemed like petty lies at the time of

discussion, went on for over 50[+] years, and

nobody has come forward – officially.

Therefore, in my opinion, such lies that they

believe had been laid to rest, must be explained,

from every point in time. Which, basically

means, there's too much explaining to deal with

questions, that _they_ feel, isn't worth the breath!

So, why do they lie in the first place?

Power? Control? Both? I think it's obvious

that, since they never explained our true history, nor have they taught us what our true purpose is, or even, that we live in a world, created by some other entity.... Well, what all this boils down to, is *We're on a Need-To-Know, basis...AND WE DON'T NEED TO KNOW-SO THEY STRONGLY BELIEVE!*

If I am right about any of this, can you imagine if they came forth and revealed this to the public? The meltdown of the vast "world's" population would collapse...

Chapter 11

The main thing I would like for you all to reconsider about living on earth, is perception. You know that message in your side mirror on your vehicle…? "Objects may appear closer…" Yeah, that message. What if it is just talking about your vehicle? What if, it's a subliminal message about life, and everything that surrounds us?

In the past few years, technology has been bringing things into perspective for many of us. Others, are blindly looking thru life, as though, they forgot to remove the 'lens-cap.'

[82]

Nevertheless, many have succumb to the idea, which of course, *objects are closer than they appear.*

For a few examples, a man in Michigan, who lives near the river between Michigan & Canada, can clearly see the country from his house by using a normal, 1080p, digital camera. In full-zoom, you can easily see the country from across the river, as though it's only a mile or so away…. Which, in a simple *Google Search*, it's literally 28 miles apart. Therefore, in retrospect, you shouldn't see *as clear as day*, with a simple {everyday camera}, that clearly.

Meaning, it shouldn't appear in a camera, only a mile away!

Another example with objects being closer than they appear… Well, this is where it becomes tricky.

The clouds are closer than expressed, and taught to us. The Sun, the 'moon,' and there's something about the stars, that humanity has always theorized, so much about. I strongly believe that stars aren't stars. In my opinion, I think that the stars are lights. Because when you have a visual from the first portion of the atmosphere, from perhaps a satellite, the stars aren't there. NASA officials claim that it's the lens' curvature. I think, they're either an illusion, or possibility, a reflection of lights coming from our own lights. There is a few theories that it could be concluded with, by me, and others. Nevertheless, there is something off in the sky above us, and that is probably why throughout history with humanity, we've always gazed into the sky. Almost as though, our inner-self is attempting to express, "your living in a fake world!"

[86]

Chapter 12

Being part of the unemployment in New York, sucks! Nonetheless, it is forcing me to become an observer, once again. And with being an observer, you begin to theorize more than if you were working.

Here is the thing. I have been made aware from talking to a friend – stuck in NYC (not me) – and he said that a ton of this Coronavirus scare, is mainly power-trip with the government. Yes, more political gain!

I was aware that much of this is one of a few things.

1) The government needed to take back

the power of the people.

2) The social distancing helps their

agenda by separation, as it has been a

plan in play, for nearly a decade – and

this forces it into overdrive!

3) Everything is a test!

Back in the 1930s, *H.G. WELLS', **WAR**

OF THE WORLDS,* had aired on a radio

station. People that tuned in late, didn't hear

that it was part of a story. These people that

panicked were from New York City (always

seems to be the epicenter of large events), New

Jersey, and a few other local states nearby.

That was a test – in my opinion – from the

government, and/or military, to see how the

populous would react to such a scenario. Guess

what, folks: ***WE FAILED!*** Miserably, in fact.

Then, in the 1960s, we went to war with

Vietnam. This war was a waste of our

countries time, and peoples lives. Many died,

many. However, if you really investigate it,

there was a CIA operation, just south of

Vietnam. This supposed operation named, The

Phoenix Program.

The Phoenix Program's purpose was to

identify, destroy, infiltrate, torture, capture,

counter-terrorism, interrogate, and assignation of the Viet Cong. The Phoenix Program was premised on the idea that the infiltration had required local support from non-combat civilian populations, what was referred to as "political branch" that had purportedly coordinated the insurgency. There were a couple of conspiracy theories that surrounded this.

The first theory was that it was conspiracy to steal/hijack the countries opium seeds. The other theory, which can sound far-fetched, was to take down a Giant. This isn't the first time that using a war to cover-up taking down a Giant is believed to occur. Only a few years ago, did our US military is believed to take down a giant that was hiding in the mountains in Afghanistan. Some believe that these mountains were the same location where *Obama Bin Laden* was to secretly been hiding. Ironic, isn't it? If you investigate *Giants*, archeologists have recovered many remains of Giants over the past century. Therefore, in my opinion, it isn't all that far-fetched. How often has our military covered-up Aliens, flying saucers, ghosts, and so much more, that they feed Hollywood to camouflage?

With the way our world leaders had shut-down (suspended) the way of the world, as we once knew, and lived (just a few months ago),

wouldn't it make perfect sense, that it's a test

(or a testament) toward the civilians?

Within the first month (March 2020), it

seemed that mass hysteria only had to do with

purchasing toilet paper (still funny), Lysol

spray and wipes, and other various cleaning

wipes – such being, flushable wipes (a.k.a., ass

wipes).

Everyone was highly encouraged (in

some cases, forced) to self-isolate [a.k.a., self-

quarantine]. Further, many states (I don't care

what some people claim), have curfews for

non-essential workers. These exist, because I

know people have received fines for being out past 8 p.m. My cousin, and others will argue until you go deaf in your ears, that there isn't, and never was a curfew. If that were true, then *essential* workers wouldn't have paperwork from their employment to show to police, if stopped. Fines could range between $100-$1500, depending on how many times you were stopped, and if it were with a group – another words, if you weren't practicing 'social distancing'. The curfew in New York State (at least Central NY), is 8:00 p.m. – 5:00 a.m.

If this was all just a test, it would make perfect sense, to me, at least. Just think about all the rules that they implemented into society.

1) Social distancing

2) Face masks

3) Gloves

4) Curfew

5) No large groups

6) Staying away from people that don't live in your own residence – this includes friends & family

7) Washing your hands frequently

8) Avoid touching your face

9) Depend on your unemployment from

your state

10)   Depend on the stimulus package of

approximately $1200 per adult –

amount changes with income and

children under 17 years of age.

There are 10 new laws/dependency upon

your government. That's nuts, in only a month.

I agree, that this virus is real, however, the

numbers aren't staggering; and it isn't from

social distancing, or any other various

precaution. I believe that people that are weak

were meant to get sick with the virus. Haven't

you heard the saying, *"Only the strong will survive?"* This is quite true, this year!

In December 2019, America's deficit was $318.9 billion. Now, add an extra $2 Trillion – we're never going to get out of debt! The following is an interesting set of statistics for y'all; from <u>www.worldometers.info/</u>

United States

Coronavirus Cases:

734,846

Deaths:

38,779

Recovered:

106,197

New York (being the epicenter) has 241,041

cases. 7,090 new cases (4.18.20), 17,671

deaths, with 540 today with said date; active

cases of 199,486; with a total of 596,532 tests

(this is as of 4/18/2020).

Under Health (same website, worldwide

numbers):

3,865,640 <u>Communicable diseases deaths</u>

144,848 <u>Seasonal Flu Deaths</u>

2,263,418 <u>Deaths of children under 5</u>

12,658,364 <u>Abortions</u>

92,040 <u>Deaths of mothers during birth year</u>

41,723,590 <u>HIV/AIDS infected people</u>

500,586 <u>Deaths caused by HIV/AIDS</u>

2,445,644 <u>Deaths caused by cancer</u>

292,088 <u>Deaths caused by Malaria</u>

11,287,700,000+ <u>Cigarettes smoked today</u>

1,488,623 <u>Deaths caused by smoking</u>

744,782 <u>Deaths caused by alcohol</u> (remember they found that Alcohol is an Essential Business)

319,329 <u>SUICIDES</u>

$119,129,300,000+ <u>SPEND ON ILLEGAL DRUGS</u>

401,982 <u>Road traffic accident deaths</u>

TOTAL COVID-19 CASES WORLDWIDE:

2,322,959; DEATHS WORLDWIDE: 159,690

RECOVERED 595,381, CURRENT

INFECTED: 1,567,888

The numbers are incredibly low, and with viewing suicide death-rates, and HIV/AIDS infected, and deaths alike, along with cancer-related-deaths, why is the world so concerned with this COVID-19?

<u>You must ask yourself, and question</u>

<u>everything!</u>

[100]

<u>**Thanks for reading, please be kind**</u>

<u>**enough to leave a review!**</u>

Further, be on the look out for

volume 2, coming soon, to an online book

retailer near you – or a click away! LOL.

Keep in mind, I have over 75 books published on Amazon.com/. Keep reading, because, after all, ***knowledge is power!***

www.ingramcontent.com/pod-product-compliance
Lightning Source LLC
Chambersburg PA
CBHW031139250726
48655CB00002B/746